MW00464454

Genre Tall Tale

Essential Question
What kinds of stories do we tell?
Why do we tell them?

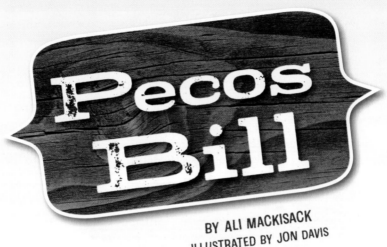

BY ALI MACKISACK
ILLUSTRATED BY JON DAVIS

CHAPTER ONE
THE EARLY YEARS OF
Pecos Bill

From the moment Pecos Bill was born, his mom felt there was something mighty special about this new baby. And she was right.

At one month old, he was already talking. By three months, Bill was walking on his own. He would wander away from his parents' homestead in Texas to wrestle with bear cubs and mountain lions until it was time for his supper. He was one for adventure, that little fellow—make no mistake.

Now, you'd think there was plenty of room out west for Bill and his 18 brothers and sisters, wouldn't you? But when other settlers set up a homestead a little more than 50 miles away, Bill's father decided the place was getting too crowded. So, quick as you like, the family loaded up the wagon and set off to find someplace where they'd have a bit more elbow room.

Well, the way they tell it, that wagon hit a rock in the middle of the Pecos River. Little Bill, who was sleeping in the back, was flung right clear of the wagon. He landed on the bank 12 miles downstream. His brothers and sisters were making so much noise that nobody heard little Bill yell. By the time they came back to look for him, little Bill was gone.

Seide Preir/Photodisc/Getty Images

You see, an old daddy coyote who happened to be passing by felt sorry for this hairless, two-legged critter. The coyote took Bill back with him to live with his pack. So Bill spent the first 15 years of his life running with the coyotes and having a grand old time. He loved to yip, howl, and hunt with them. Pretty soon, he could out-hunt and out-howl any coyote in the whole Southwest. Pecos Bill just about believed he was a coyote himself.

As Pecos Bill grew, he became stronger, smarter, and faster than any other critter on the continent. He never saw another human being in those coyote years.

Then one day, a cowboy came riding through the sagebrush. The cowboy couldn't believe his eyes. In front of him was a young man surrounded by a pack of yipping coyotes. The young man was wrestling a bear—and winning.

"Who are you?" asked the cowboy.

It was a long time since Bill had heard human language. It took him a while to get used to hearing it and speaking it again.

"Well, I'm a coyote," he said at last.

The cowboy laughed. "You are no coyote," he said. "You're a man."

"But I have fleas, and I howl at the moon," replied Bill.

"That doesn't prove anything," the cowboy said. "Most folk in Texas have fleas and howl at the moon. And besides, coyotes have bushy tails."

Bill peered around behind him and saw that the cowboy was right. He had no bushy tail.

So Bill decided he must be human after all. He took the cowboy up on his offer to teach him cowboy ways. Pecos Bill thanked the coyotes who had raised him. Then he borrowed some boots, chaps, and other riding clothes from the cowboy and set off running along beside the cowboy's horse.

Before they had gone far, a 15-foot rattlesnake reared up from behind a pile of rocks. Pecos Bill narrowed his eyes. "I'll let you have the first bite, rattler," he said. "That seems only fair, but after that, I'm going to teach you how to behave."

And that's just what Bill did. After the snake's first strike, he spun that snake around in the air until it was twice as long and four times as skinny. Then he wound it up, hung it over his shoulder, and ran to catch up with the cowboy.

Next a mountain lion leaped out at them. The cowboy's horse reared up, threw its rider, and galloped away. Pecos Bill grabbed that mountain lion, wrestled it to the ground, and leaped on its back to chase after the horse. Then Bill took hold of the snake hanging from his shoulder, and holding on to its tail, swung it in the air until its long body made a loop. Finally, he threw the looped snake over the horse's head and pulled tight.

The cowboy's jaw dropped to the ground when he saw Pecos Bill return with the horse. "I've never seen anything like it," he gasped.

"That's because nobody invented the lasso before," said Bill, winding the snake back up around his arm.

CHAPTER TWO

Pecos Bill, COWBOY

As they crossed the prairie, the cowboy told Bill that where they were headed was no place for weak or tender folks. It was a territory where the men were so tough that they crushed rocks with their teeth and ate bent nails for their supper. But that kind of country posed no problem for Pecos Bill. He thought that it sounded like just the place for him.

At the first cowboy camp they came to, Pecos Bill made himself right at home. He sauntered into the campsite, ate some beans, drank some coffee, and then picked his teeth with a cactus spine.

(t) Seide Preis/Photodisc/Getty Images

6

"Who's the boss around here?" he asked.

A giant of a man lurched to his feet. "Well, I was," he said. He glanced from the rattlesnake to the mountain lion and then back at Bill. "But you are now," he added.

"Good," said Bill, and he set about inventing the art of being a cowboy.

He invented spurs and cowboy songs and ten-gallon hats. He invented critters such as centipedes for playing practical jokes on the other cowboys. He tied strips of rawhide together so that all the cowboys could have lassos. Then Bill practiced with his own rattler lasso. Soon he could lasso the wing feathers off an eagle.

When he found out that the ranchers had so few cattle because they couldn't catch them, he lassoed an entire herd of longhorns in one loop. Soon the ranchers had so many cattle that they couldn't keep them together. So Bill invented fence posts, hitching rails, and cattle branding.

Bill's own Texas ranch soon got so big that he staked out New Mexico as his front pasture and fenced off Arizona for raising his calves. Tired of carrying water from the Gulf of California, he used his bare hands to dig out the Rio Grande.

When the time came to find a horse, Pecos Bill went after a wild palomino stallion that everyone talked about, but nobody could catch.

He tracked the palomino from Texas to Montana and back again, running all the way. Then he planted himself in a narrow canyon with towering cliffs on either side and waited. When the stallion galloped into view, Bill jumped out.

The stallion was so surprised to see Pecos Bill appear in front of him that he jammed his legs straight and slid to a halt. He had been galloping so fast that he got stuck in his own skid furrow. Pecos Bill leaped on the horse's back and held on. By the time Bill pulled the stallion free, that horse was broken in.

Bill was the only man the stallion would let ride on its back. Every other cowboy who tried to ride him was flung so high he was never seen again. Bill named that horse Widow Maker.

Widow Maker was Bill's pride and joy. However, the horse also brought him trouble like never before. You see, Pecos Bill fell in love with a woman named Slue-Foot Sue. She said she would only marry Bill if he let her ride Widow Maker.

Slue-Foot Sue sure was a good rider—nearly as good as Pecos Bill himself. The first time Pecos Bill saw her, Slue-Foot Sue was riding a catfish as big as a whale down the Rio Grande. She was standing on that old catfish's back, holding on with one hand and firing her six-shooter into the clouds with the other.

In that instant, Pecos Bill knew that this was the woman for him. He wasn't happy about her wanting to ride Widow Maker, but he knew he had to let her or she wouldn't marry him.

Right after they had said their wedding vows and posed for a wedding photograph, Slue-Foot Sue jumped on Widow Maker's back.

Well, that horse did what that horse always did. He commenced bucking as if he'd sat on a cactus, until he threw his rider 40 miles straight up.

But Slue-Foot Sue was wearing something called a bustle in the back of her wedding gown. Now, a bustle is a kind of frame that women back in those days wore under their dresses. It helped their dresses keep a nice shape. And it was a mighty good thing Sue was wearing one. When she came down, she just sprang on up again. Up, down, up, down— Slue-Foot Sue kept right on bouncing on her bustle.

No one knows for sure what happened next. Some folk say that she just kept on bouncing, blowing kisses to her man every time she came down. Others say Pecos Bill lassoed Slue-Foot Sue with that old rattler lasso and they lived happily ever after.

CHAPTER THREE

Pecos Bill
AND THE TORNADO

Now, Bill could ride just about anything a man might ride. The way people tell it, the only time he ever got himself thrown was when he rode a tornado.

It all started up near Kansas during the worst drought that had ever been seen in those parts. The ground was so dry that a man would step in a crack and not stop falling for three days. The cows and horses got so dried up that whenever there was a puff of wind, they'd blow clean away unless they were tied down. It would be no exaggeration to say that even the cactuses were packing up and heading east.

So when Pecos Bill saw a mean old tornado heading his way, he figured he'd have some fun and do some good, too. He knew there was water inside that towering twister, and he aimed to get it.

The tornado was the biggest anyone had ever seen. It turned the sky dark purple and green, and it roared like a lion. But that didn't worry Bill.

Seide Preis/Photodisc/Getty Images

He climbed up a tree and then called to the tornado to come on over and say howdy. He was planning to jump on its back as soon as it got close enough. But when he saw how high that funnel was, he knew he'd have to think of something else.

Then lightning struck, and Bill got a bright idea.

Quick as a flash, he bolted out of the tree and grabbed hold of that lightning. It flung him halfway to the sun. On his way down, he landed clean on the shoulders of that tornado. His ten-gallon hat was only slightly crooked on his head.

Well, having some old cowboy sitting on it didn't impress that twister at all. It bucked and twisted and tried to shake Bill loose. Bill just wrapped his legs around its belly and held on tight.

The tornado twisted rivers like a little girl's braids. It hit the ground so hard that it split open the Grand Canyon. Still it couldn't get rid of its rider. Bill just flung his lasso around the tornado and pulled.

Being squeezed like that, the tornado spat out rivers and rain onto the parched ground below. Bill kept pulling the lasso, trying to wring every last drop of water out of that tornado.

He rode across three states, bringing the drought in all of them to a fast finish. By the time he reached California, that mean old twister was worn out.

Bill let the tornado sink to its knees, but the tornado gave one last buck, and off Bill flew. He hit the dirt with such a thump that he moved thousands of acres of rock and sand, creating the basin they call Death Valley.

And that's how the rodeo began, though most folks stick to riding bucking broncos instead of tornadoes these days.

There are all kinds of tales told about Pecos Bill and his deeds. It seems that nobody can agree on the facts for any of them, including the story of how he died. Most folks, however, think it goes something like this ...

Pecos Bill got older, but he could still out-ride, out-shoot, and out-holler any cowboy. One day when he was walking along a sidewalk in town, he saw a city slicker who had just arrived in cowboy country. The man thought he was quite the cowboy. His fancy cowboy outfit didn't fool anybody, though. It had not a speck of dust on it anywhere.

Pecos Bill took one look at this fancy-pants cowboy and started to laugh. The man heard him laughing and tried to swagger into a saloon. Well, that was just too much for Pecos Bill. He laughed so hard that he couldn't stand up. He had to lie down on the sidewalk to laugh some more. And that's how he died, see.

He laughed himself to death.

Respond to Reading

Summarize

Use the most important details from the story to summarize *Pecos Bill*. Your graphic organizer may help you.

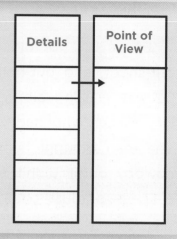

Details	Point of View

Text Evidence

1. How can you tell that *Pecos Bill* is a tall tale? Give details about the characters and events. **GENRE**

2. What does the narrator think of Pecos Bill? Give at least two examples of descriptions that show this. **POINT OF VIEW**

3. What does the word *tough* mean on page 6? Use context clues and an antonym in the paragraph to help you. **SYNONYMS AND ANTONYMS**

4. Write about the narrator's view of the tornado. **WRITE ABOUT READING**

Compare Texts

Read a legend about an amazing fountain.

THE FOUNTAIN OF YOUTH

In the year 1513, Spanish explorer Juan Ponce de León was sailing toward the New World. He was hoping to discover the land of Beimeni and claim it for the Spanish king.

Beimeni was said to be a land of beauty and wealth. If he found it, Ponce de León would be granted the right to govern it on behalf of the Spanish king.

Ponce de León had heard a legend about a special pool of water called the Fountain of Youth. According to the legend, anyone who drank from or bathed in the Fountain of Youth became young again.

On board his sailing ship, the explorer pondered the story. Could it be true? Perhaps the Fountain of Youth might be found in the yet unexplored land of Beimeni.

Illustration: Juan Caminador

Ponce de León let his mind drift off as he imagined what it would be like to find the legendary fountain.

In ancient times, Alexander the Great had spoken of a miraculous "sweet water" spring. His warriors had bathed in the spring and become young. Perhaps the fountain was in the Middle East?

Others were certain the fountain was in Ethiopia. And someone had told Ponce de León a recent tale about an Arawak chief from Cuba. As the story went, the chief had sailed north with a band of adventurers and never returned. Perhaps these men were living, forever young, beside the Fountain of Youth in the beautiful land of Beimeni?

Many believed the Fountain of Youth was somewhere in the New World, which had been charted by Columbus. They thought that it was only a matter of time before a heroic explorer discovered it. Ponce de León wanted to be that explorer so much that he could hardly sleep.

One day, Ponce de León's lookout began shouting and pointing as he peered at something through his spyglass. He handed the spyglass to Ponce de León. There, right where the navigators had plotted it on the charts, was a beautiful land covered in a rainbow of flowers.

Illustration: Juan Caminador

"Beimeni," Ponce de León gasped.

But Ponce de León's crew had not found the Fountain of Youth. Instead, they had discovered a place they named La Florida, now known as Florida.

Today the Fountain of Youth Archaeological Park is located where Ponce de León landed on the Florida coast.

As for the Fountain of Youth, it is still waiting to be discovered.

POSTSCRIPT

Ponce de León was a real person. There is little historical evidence to link him to the search for the Fountain of Youth. However, over time, his name, the legendary fountain, and his landing on the shore of Florida have become so entwined that the story has become a legend.

Make Connections

Why do you think people create legends to explain nature or natural events? **ESSENTIAL QUESTION**

How are the stories about Pecos Bill and Ponce de León similar? How are they different? **TEXT TO TEXT**

Focus on Genre

Tall Tales Tall tales are stories about people who have exaggerated abilities. These tales often highlight qualities that are valued in a culture, such as physical strength or self-confidence. Sometimes a tall tale may be based on the life of a real person, but his or her feats are exaggerated beyond what could really be true.

Read and Find As Pecos Bill grows, his life and exploits become more and more incredible. These are described using exaggerated comparisons; for example, he could "lasso the wing feathers off an eagle." (page 7)

Your Turn

What abilities do you value? Make a list of several of these abilities. For example, you might list scoring well on computer games, soccer skills, and dance moves.

Next, choose at least three of these abilities and for each one, write an exaggerated comparison to describe a person who has this ability. For example, "She could dribble the ball right around the moon and back in the blink of an eye."

Illustrate one of your ideas and share it with the class.